Poetry Writing

BY
REBECCA DYE, Ph.D.

COPYRIGHT © 2001 Mark Twain Media, Inc.

ISBN 1-58037-178-7

Printing No. CD-1399

Mark Twain Media, Inc., Publishers
Distributed by Carson-Dellosa Publishing Company, Inc.

The purchase of this book entitles the buyer to reproduce the student pages for classroom use only. Other permissions may be obtained by writing Mark Twain Media, Inc., Publishers.

All rights reserved. Printed in the United States of America.

Table of Contents

Introduction to Teachers 1
Introduction to Students 2

Part I: What Does It Take to Make a Poem? 3
   Chapter One: *Rhythmic Language* 3
      Metrical Patterns
   Chapter Two: *Condensed, Concentrated Language* 7
      Metaphor, Personification, Simile
   Chapter Three: *Rhyming Language* 11
      A Reminder to Avoid Plagiarism

Part II: Kinds of Poems 14
   Chapter Four: *Couplets and Tercets and Short Stanzas* 14
   Chapter Five: *The Clerihew* 20
   Chapter Six: *The Ballad* 24
   Chapter Seven: *Concrete Poems* 30
   Chapter Eight: *The Limerick* 33
   Chapter Nine: *The Sonnet* 37
   Chapter Ten: *The Haiku* 46
   Chapter Eleven: *The Biopoem* 48
   Chapter Twelve: *The Cinquain* 51
   Chapter Thirteen: *Blank Verse* 53
   Chapter Fourteen: *Free Verse* 55

Part III: Starting and Finishing Your Work 56
   Chapter Fifteen: *Looking for Ideas and Words That Work* 56
      Onomatopoeic Words
   Chapter Sixteen: *Revising and Editing* 61

Introduction to Teachers

Including poetry writing in the language arts curriculum gives teachers the chance to encourage and assist students as they discover and use their imaginations. However, neither competent writers nor their completed poems appear on demand. Taking ideas and turning them into satisfying poems with attention to form (metrical details and rhyme patterns) as well as use of language (metaphor, simile, and personification) is difficult, but rewarding, work. Helping someone else try to do this is equally difficult and rewarding.

I have written this book to supplement your school's writing curriculum, not to replace it. My approach involves asking students to become more sensitive to language itself before they begin to write their poems. I do this through several short writing activities that can be completed individually or through whole-class instruction. I then present a variety of poetic forms and present examples to show just how certain kinds of poems are constructed. I also discuss the matter of plagiarism: stealing others' words and work. Students need to understand and appreciate the value of honesty in all parts of their academic lives.

Sometimes I invite students to write with me to gain a sense of what cooperative writing is like. I also ask students to copy some of their best work onto pages in this book. I make this suggestion so students will not lose their work, and hopefully, they will have an opportunity to go back later to revisit and revise their work.

Finally, I ask students to return to thinking about words, to listening to the sounds of words, and to learning new ways of saying the most common yet, often, the most interesting things we know. My suggestions on editing are brief because, depending on how you assign these types of writing projects, you will want and need to satisfy a number of curricular goals.

Please encourage your students to try writing poems. In the process, they can become more proficient in their use of language, more sensitive to the power of words, and more interested in hearing and reading the works of others.

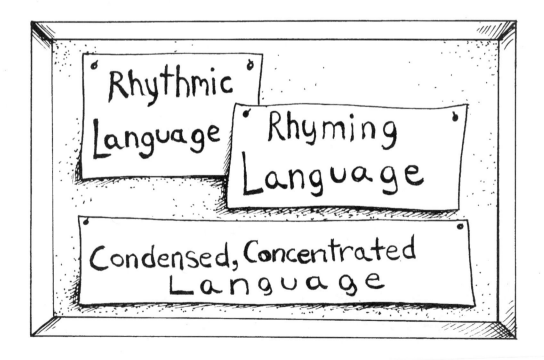

Introduction to Students

This book is about poems and how real writers—just like you and me—go about writing them. Sometimes we write poems as a way to celebrate special events. We write poems to share with our families and friends. These are what I call *public poems.* Sometimes we write poems because we feel *very:* very happy, very sad, very upset, and even very confused. Many times, our *very* poems are written just for ourselves and no one else. By writing them, we can get all those jumbled feelings out where we can sort through them and see them more clearly. It doesn't always mean that we can change things, but it just seems to make us feel better when we can wrap words around feelings, take them out of our minds, and look at them for a while. Our *very* poems are usually *private poems* because they are usually written and read *in private.* Both kinds of poems are good because both kinds can make us think and feel better. While you may want to do some of the poems suggested in this book for yourself, you will probably be doing most of these as parts of assignments from your teachers.

Most real poets write poems all the time, starting and stopping, searching for a better word, and looking around for just the right phrase. They keep their poems in notebooks or folders so they can go back to them and read them again. Now, you'll never guess what they do when they read them in the future! They usually grab their pencils and start changing things again—a word here and a comma there—until everything is just *so.* Real poets don't always like to write poems, but they just can't help it.

And yes, you are a poet! You often struggle with words to wrap around your feelings of being proud and happy, sad and afraid, excited and calm, certain and confused. You are a poet because you enjoy playing with words that not only mean something in a sentence but also have interesting sounds and rhythms. When no one is looking or listening, you like to say those words out loud, rolling them around the space between your ears, swishing them around in your mouth, and spitting them out into thin air. You are a poet because sometimes you don't like to write poems, but you just can't help it. You are a poet because you really do have something to say, and the rest of us would very much like to hear it.

Chapter One: *Rhythmic Language*

If you asked ten people what a poem is, you would probably end up with ten different responses. If you took ten different dictionaries and looked up the word *poetry* in each of them, you would probably find ten different definitions. However, each person's response and each definition from those ten dictionaries would probably have several things in common.

One thing each definition would probably mention is that poetry is *rhythmic language.* It is true that many poems do have a regular kind of rhythm or **beat** or **meter/metrical pattern**, as people who study and write poetry might say. Poetry does have rhythm because poetry is built word by word, and every word has some kind of rhythm.

Words have rhythm?
Yes! They sure do!

Words have rhythm inside them, and when you start putting those words together with other words, you can create some very interesting combinations.

Yes, but how do words have rhythm inside them?

Words have rhythm made by their patterns of accented as well as unaccented syllables. If a word had only one syllable and was standing alone, it would be accented. For example, each of these words would be accented.

the

dog

saw

the

cat

Now, if you put the words together to make a sentence, and if you read that sentence aloud, you would probably emphasize (stress or accent) some words and not emphasize (not accent) others. For example, you might read the sentence this way.

(Read the next sentence out loud and put some emphasis on the underlined words.)

The <u>dog</u> saw the <u>cat</u>.

On its own, each word still has only one syllable with one accent. Putting them together, you have created a rhythm pattern. You don't believe me? Try this.

If a word is NOT underlined (accented), call it *daw*.
If a word IS underlined (accented), call it *dee*.

Chapter One: *Rhythmic Language*

The <u>dog</u> saw the <u>cat</u>. That sentence has now become *daw dee daw daw dee,* and you can keep that rhythm (beat) going by adding other sentences that are made up of words having only one syllable each.

The dog saw the cat.	(daw dee daw daw dee)
The cat saw the bird.	(daw dee daw daw dee)
The bird saw the worm.	(daw dee daw daw dee)
The worm saw the bug.	(daw dee daw daw dee)
The bug saw the rose.	(daw dee daw daw dee)
… and on and on!	(daw dee daw dee … Oops, sorry!)

But you and I know that there are a bazillion words in the dictionary that have more than one syllable. If you look up one of those words with more than one syllable, you will see that the dictionary will tell you which syllable is accented and which is unaccented. It won't say anything about *daw* and *dee!* It will just mark a syllable as / (accented) or *u* (unaccented). Sometimes the dictionary will just mark the accented syllable, so you know the rest are unaccented. Here are a few examples.

$$\text{butterfly} = \overset{/}{\text{but}}\ \overset{u}{\text{ter}}\ \overset{u}{\text{fly}} \qquad \text{peanut} = \overset{/}{\text{pea}}\ \overset{u}{\text{nut}} \qquad \text{pioneer} = \overset{u}{\text{pi}}\ \overset{u}{\text{o}}\ \overset{/}{\text{neer}}$$

$$\text{amount} = \overset{u}{\text{a}}\ \overset{/}{\text{mount}} \qquad \text{hobo} = \overset{/}{\text{ho}}\ \overset{/}{\text{bo}}$$

These five patterns are the standard rhythm patterns found in most poetry. Each pattern has a particular name that people who study and write poems like to use. For example, if a word has a pattern like *amount* or *about* or *around* (*u /* or *daw dee*), we would say the pattern is an **iambus**. A word like *peanut* or *sandwich* or *rainbow* has just the opposite pattern: */ u* (*dee daw*). That pattern is a **trochee**. Words having three syllables and accented like *butterfly* or *merrily* (*dee daw daw*) have a pattern called a **dactyl**. Words like *lemonade* or *pioneer* (*daw daw dee*) have a pattern called an **anapest**. Words like *hobo* or *football* (*/ /* or *dee dee*) have a pattern called a **spondee**.

For right now, just remember that words really do have rhythm inside them.

Poetry Writing   Chapter One: *Rhythmic Language*

Name: _____ Date: _____

Chapter One: *Rhythmic Language*

Just for fun, how many words can you think of that have these kinds of accent/unaccent patterns?

butterfly	peanut	pioneer	amount	hobo
_____	_____	_____	_____	_____
_____	_____	_____	_____	_____
_____	_____	_____	_____	_____
_____	_____	_____	_____	_____
_____	_____	_____	_____	_____
_____	_____	_____	_____	_____
_____	_____	_____	_____	_____
_____	_____	_____	_____	_____
_____	_____	_____	_____	_____

Congratulations!!! You have just become word wacky!

Now remember, when we put those individual words in sentences, we don't always follow the accent/unaccent patterns exactly. We often emphasize key words to show they are important. For example, look at these sentences.

The <u>hobo</u> saw the <u>butterfly</u>.
The   hobo   saw   the   butterfly.
(daw dee-dee daw daw dee-daw-daw)

The <u>peanuts</u> had just the <u>right</u> <u>amount</u> of <u>salt</u>.
The   peanuts   had   just   the   right   amount   of   salt.
(daw dee-daw daw daw daw dee daw-dee daw dee)

<u>We</u> <u>went</u> to the pioneer <u>museum</u> on <u>vacation</u>.
We   went   to   the   pioneer   museum   on   vacation.
(dee dee daw daw daw-daw-dee daw-dee-daw daw daw-dee-daw)

The sentence *The hobo saw the butterfly* has a kind of beat/rhythm to it. (If you read the sentence out loud three times, you will begin to hear and feel it.) The sentence *The peanuts had just the right amount of salt* does not have a repeating beat in it, and it is too long to repeat it to make one. (Don't believe me? Try saying it out loud three times and see for yourself!) The sentence *We went to the pioneer museum on vacation* doesn't really have a beginning-of-the-sentence-to-end pattern, but it begins to feel like a pattern when it starts the *museum on vacation* part.

© Mark Twain Media, Inc., Publishers

Name: _____   Date: _____

Chapter One: *Rhythmic Language*

So, our words really do have rhythm! Individual words can have rhythm, and words put together into sentences can have a rhythm. Sometimes the rhythm is smooth and repeats over and over. Sometimes it is lumpy and bumpy because no particular pattern repeats itself.

Look at these sentences. Underline the words that you think are the key words to emphasize (accent) in the sentence, and see if you find smooth patterns that repeat or just lumpy/bumpy beats. (Mark the words with *u* and / or *daw* and *dee* if that is easier for you.)

1. I know I saw Mark at the movies.

2. She said she'd be back in ten minutes.

3. They had a big sale on pancake syrup, flour, and frozen peas.

4. Bob invited Bill, Bill invited Ed, Ed invited Lee, and Lee invited Jim.

5. They ate hamburgers and French fries for dinner.

6. Jerry said something really funny.

7. First it rained, and then it snowed.

8. His shirt was bright green, and his shorts were bright blue.

Which words did you emphasize? How might the pattern change if you emphasized a different word? Take a few minutes to discover how other people read and emphasize words in the sentences. Do they stress the same words you originally chose? (Were their rhythm patterns different from yours?)

As I said at the beginning of this chapter, poetry is usually described as having rhythmic language. Most poems do have some kind of regular or repeating rhythm, but there is one kind of poem that does not have a regular rhythm. That kind has no regular beat, and what's more, it has no words that rhyme. It is called **free verse**. We will be writing some free verse in a later chapter in this book.

Well, if free verse doesn't have a regular beat and has no words that rhyme, what does it have that makes it a poem? Isn't it just like every other sentence?

Good question!

Free verse depends on the same thing upon which every other poem depends: condensed language that expresses attitudes, moods, and different ways of thinking about something.

Chapter Two: *Condensed, Concentrated Language*

Is condensed language anything like condensed milk, condensed soup, or concentrated orange juice?

Yes, exactly! Poems try to say in a few words what others say in several sentences. By carefully choosing just a few of the right words, the poet will not just describe a situation but will tell you how he/she thinks and feels about it.

For example, this might be the official weather forecast.

The weather tomorrow will be a mix of snow, freezing rain, and sleet. Wind gusts of up to 30 miles per hour will make travel hazardous. With gusts that strong, we can expect wind chills to be down to 10 degrees below zero.

These are all factual details that the weather person might announce. But a poet might deliver the forecast like this using condensed language.

Stinging winds of icy snow try tricks not treats on feet and
tires. It's ten below! Stay warm. Go slow. Stay home.

Let's say this is the forecast: *The weather for today will be sunny with highs around 80 degrees and the low around 65. The winds will be light and variable, and the humidity will be low.* Try using condensed language to describe not just the facts, but also how you feel about a day like that.

Me? I like meatloaf, but you might not like it at all. Simply saying, "I don't like meatloaf." isn't a very convincing or powerful way to say it. Remember, poetry uses concentrated, powerful language to describe as well as to explain. So a poetic way of saying that *I like meatloaf* might be like this.

It even smells delicious! Meatloaf is that miracle mixture of meat and spice, crackers, ketchup, and Mom's special touch.

A more powerful way to say that you don't like meatloaf might be …

With one whiff, I start to gag. Meatloaf is a fatal collision of cracker crumbs, raw egg, onions, and mystery meat, sinking fast in an oil slick of ketchup.

Sometimes the best way to describe something is to call it something else. Did you notice that in the first example about meatloaf, I called it a *miracle mixture* because miracle makes me think of things that are beautiful and wonderful and perfect. I tried to use several words starting with "m" because when I really like something, I sometimes say "M-m-m-m good!" In the second example, I called it a *fatal collision*—something truly awful and sickening. I wrote *cracker crumbs collide* because I wanted the reader to hear a crashing, out-of-control noise like a car wreck when looking at that meatloaf. I also decided to call it mystery meat, not because it is "M-m-m-m good," but because it is "Hmm-m-m … what is it?" (You just can't tell what it is by looking at it!)

Poetry Writing   Chapter Two: *Condensed, Concentrated Language*

Name: _____   Date: _____

Chapter Two: *Condensed, Concentrated Language*

We all know that meatloaf is neither a miracle nor a car wreck. However, by hearing it called something different from what we expect, we begin to see it, smell it, taste it, and even touch it in a more powerful way. When we call one thing something else so we can compare the two things, we create something called a **metaphor**. We use metaphors all the time to describe common things in a different way! For example, have you ever heard a car that never seems to work right called a *lemon*? Does that mean your car has suddenly turned into a piece of yellow citrus fruit? Of course not! Has anyone ever called you a *turkey*?

1. What does it really mean if someone says a person is a **turkey**?
   _____
   _____

2. a **hot dog**?
   _____
   _____

3. a **cool cat**?
   _____
   _____

4. a **pillar of the community**?
   _____
   _____

5. a **fountain of ideas**?
   _____
   _____

6. a **real** *nut*?
   _____
   _____

By using just a few words, a metaphor can say so much!

© Mark Twain Media, Inc., Publishers

Chapter Two: *Condensed, Concentrated Language*

Another way that poems use language powerfully is to describe things that are not alive as if they were living creatures. They are described like they were people or persons. We call this **personification**.

For example, how are these nonhuman things given human characteristics? What do these mean?

1. the nose of an aircraft _____

2. the eye of the storm _____

3. the eye of the needle _____

4. the foot of the mountain _____

5. The White House listened to the voters. _____

6. The saw sank its teeth into the log. _____

7. The motor coughed and died. _____

8. The ice maker spit out cubes. _____

9. The chair groaned when I sat down. _____

10. The sun smiled down on us. _____

Poetry Writing　　　　　　　　　　　　　　Chapter Two: *Condensed, Concentrated Language*

Name: _____ Date: _____

Chapter Two: *Condensed, Concentrated Language*

　　Metaphor and personification are just two ways that we can say many things in just a few words. Poets find using metaphor and personification very handy because it lets them say much in few words. **Simile** is another common way to do the same thing. In a simile, you actually use the words *like* or *as* when you say what something is like or as.

You fill in the blanks.

1. The road was as smooth as _____.

2. The huge package was as light as _____.

3. That story is as old as _____.

4. My grandpa said he felt as young as _____.

5. That thief was as sly as _____.

　　These are just a few examples of simile. Most of our similes are ones we hear and have heard over and over. We know these so well that they don't make the impact (impression) they should. Try to rewrite these sentences with similes using different, fresh similes OR rewrite them using a metaphor.

6. _____

_____

7. _____

_____

8. _____

_____

9. _____

_____

10. _____

_____

© Mark Twain Media, Inc., Publishers

Poetry Writing Chapter Three: *Rhyming Language*

Name: _____ Date: _____

Chapter Three: *Rhyming Language*

The final thing that most definitions and responses about poems will have in common is that they will say most poems have **rhyme** in them. Typically, poems have words at the ends of lines that rhyme with other end-of-the-line words. Sometimes you will even find rhyme in the middle of the lines.

Words rhyme when the accented syllable's vowel (*a, e, i, o, u,* and sometimes *y*) and the consonants following that vowel set up a similar or matching sound. This pattern of creating matching sounds can happen within the line or between two or more lines of poetry.

It is fun to rhyme words. It requires a good ear, a good eye, and a sizeable vocabulary. Just how big are your ears, eyes, and vocabulary? In this game, we will stretch the rules just a bit. You can use single words or groups of words to make matching rhymes. I'll do the first few as examples.

me: tree   free   spending spree   flea   bee   fee

line: fine   spine   friend of mine   twine

mug: thug   jug   lightning bug   hug

(Now, my friends, you're on your own. Please don't whine! Please don't moan!)

1. book _____

2. load _____

3. garden _____

4. video _____

5. rake _____

6. tractor _____

Poetry Writing — Chapter Three: *Rhyming Language*

Name: _____ Date: _____

Chapter Three: *Rhyming Language*

7. valentine _____

_____

8. map _____

_____

9. potato _____

_____

10. verse _____

_____

11. turkey _____

_____

12. robin _____

_____

13. screen _____

_____

14. trunk _____

_____

15. home _____

_____

16. skirt _____

_____

Chapter Three: *Rhyming Language*

What does it take to make a poem? It takes words that are put together in a special way to give us a feeling of rhythm, to give us ideas that are stated in condensed or concentrated language, and very often, to give us a feeling of balance and connection through rhyme. But poetry is more than just that.

I think poetry is when a writer uses words and sounds and rhythms to describe and explain things in such a way that makes the reader see, hear, feel, and almost taste what the poet discusses. Poetry is when the writer creates and controls words so carefully that even the sounds of the words' letters obey the poet's wishes. Poets are powerful people, and poetry is powerful language.

In the next chapters, we will be looking at some poems I have written. We will also be trying to write some ourselves. I've put poems I've written in italics—squiggly print. When you write, you don't need to use italics, but you do need to use honesty.

Don't take what I have written and call it your work. That is called **plagiarism** (play-juh-rism), and it is basically stealing something (written words) that belongs to someone else. You may read something and get a great idea for a poem or a story, and that is wonderful. Just don't take the exact idea or exact words that someone else wrote and say that they are yours. That's what I call *grand theft lingo*.

Can you get into any real trouble stealing words? You bet. Teachers often give students who plagiarize a 0 or an F. Judges often require adults who do this to pay *h-u-g-e* fines. But even worse than all that, people will know you are a thief. Why be a thief? Just be your own creative, imaginative self!

Chapter Four: *Couplets and Tercets and Short Stanzas*

There are so many different kinds of poems that it is difficult to decide where to start. Probably the first poems that we heard as little children were **couplets**, two lines that ended with words that rhyme.

The following are examples of couplets.

There was a dog
Who ate like a hog.

My old neighbor, Billie,
Is really quite silly.

The more books I read,
The more books I need.

If I don't do my best,
I won't pass the test.

Each of these examples is really one sentence that is broken into two parts to form the two lines. These are probably the easiest to create. They are so easy that you can make them up as you jump rope—and probably have!

The cat stretched in the morning sun.
He caught his mouse. His work was done.

The car turned right into my lane.
I hit the brakes. I felt the pain.

The peanut butter, thick and sweet,
Sticks to my teeth. It's tough to eat.

These three couplets are very different from the first examples. First, each begins with a longer sentence. Then, these couplets (two lines of poetry) are groups of sentences that almost tell a kind of story—a *very tiny* story. The lines are related—the second line tells more about the first line.

I woke too early, woke too soon.
I wish I could have slept till noon.

The sky was cold and bleak and gray.
It was a sad and lonesome day.

© Mark Twain Media, Inc., Publishers

Poetry Writing — Chapter Four: *Couplets and Tercets and Short Stanzas*

Name: _____ Date: _____

Chapter Four: *Couplets and Tercets and Short Stanzas*

These couplets are different from the others as their first and second lines basically say the same thing. They are not the sing-song, rope-jumping rhymes like the first group, and they don't really describe a situation as the second examples do. One line reinforces (emphasizes) the other.

Now it is your turn to write a few couplets. Try to write at least two couplets like each of the three groups. (Caution: Use a pencil so you can easily move words around.)

Group One couplets:

1. _____
   _____
2. _____
   _____
3. _____
   _____

Group Two couplets:

1. _____
   _____
2. _____
   _____
3. _____
   _____

Group Three couplets:

1. _____
   _____
2. _____
   _____
3. _____
   _____

Poetry Writing   Chapter Four: *Couplets and Tercets and Short Stanzas*

Name: _____ Date: _____

Chapter Four: *Couplets and Tercets and Short Stanzas*

Now that we have written groups of two lines that rhyme, let's try coming up with more than two lines. Two lines that rhyme make a very short poem! Let's try writing a **stanza**: one of several groupings of lines in a poem. For example, if we wrote a poem that was ten lines long and used couplets, we would probably have five stanzas. (A stanza is usually easy to spot. There is usually a blank space separating each stanza.) If you wrote a poem with stanzas that had three lines each, you would have written **tercets**. If you wrote a poem with four lines in a stanza, you would have written what is called a **quatrain**. Here are examples of stanzas of different lengths.

Couplet: The sky was cold and bleak and gray.
                It was a sad and lonesome day.

Tercet: The sky was cold and bleak and gray.
                It was a sad and lonesome day.
                I'll have to stay inside to play.

This is also a tercet.   The sky was cold and bleak and gray.
                          The geese were flying south.
                          It was a sad and lonesome day.

There are two ways to make a tercet! A tercet can be a group of three lines with each line rhyming, or it can be a group of three lines in which the first and third lines rhyme.

Try writing one tercet with three lines that rhyme.

_____

_____

_____

Now, try writing one tercet with the first and the third lines rhyming.

_____

_____

_____

© Mark Twain Media, Inc., Publishers

Poetry Writing

Name: _____ Date: _____

Chapter Four: *Couplets and Tercets and Short Stanzas*

Now what? Right! Let's try working towards a group of four lines: a quatrain. Before you begin to write, think math. What plus what makes four? There are three possible ways to make a quatrain. You can write four lines with each line ending with the same rhyme.

Please, go away.
You can't stay.
I can't play.
Please, go away.

You can write two couplets to make four lines: 2 + 2 = 4.

Please, go away.
You can't stay.
I must study
With my buddy.

You can write four lines in which the first and third lines rhyme and the second and fourth lines rhyme. (Got that?)

Please, let me study.
Oh, please, go away.
I know you're my buddy,
But you just can't stay.

You guessed it! Now, you try writing one of each kind of quatrain.

Two Couplets: Each line should end with the same rhyme.

_____

_____

_____

_____

Two Couplets: Lines one and two rhyme, and lines three and four rhyme.

_____

_____

_____

_____

Poetry Writing • Chapter Four: *Couplets and Tercets and Short Stanzas*

Name: _____ Date: _____

Chapter Four: *Couplets and Tercets and Short Stanzas*

Four Lines: Lines one and three rhyme, and lines two and four rhyme.

_____

_____

_____

_____

    As you read more poems in your language arts and literature books, notice how those poems are usually built. Are the lines in groups of two, three, four, or even eight? How many stanzas are there in the poem? How do the lines rhyme? Are the lines rhymed in pairs, or does every other line rhyme? Think about poems that you like. If the poem has rhyming lines, which ones rhyme?

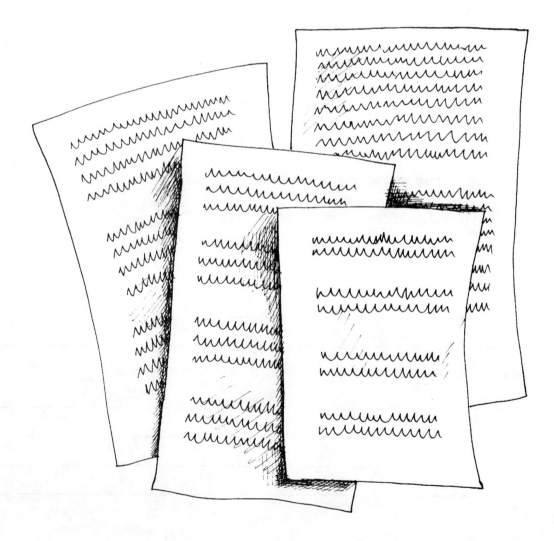

Poetry Writing   Chapter Four: *Couplets and Tercets and Short Stanzas*

Name: _____ Date: _____

Chapter Four: *Couplets and Tercets and Short Stanzas*

After writing several couplets, tercets, and quatrains, copy or attach your best efforts in the space below.

Couplets:

_____

_____

_____

_____

Tercets:

_____

_____

_____

_____

_____

_____

Quatrains:

_____

_____

_____

_____

_____

_____

_____

_____

Poetry Writing │ Chapter Five: *The Clerihew*

Name: _____ Date: _____

Chapter Five: *The Clerihew*

Now that you have thought about and written couplets and short stanzas, you are ready to try a form of poetry called a **Clerihew**. The Clerihew has one stanza of four lines. The first and second lines rhyme, and the third and fourth lines rhyme. Clerihews (invented by Edward Clerihew Bentley) are usually "light" or funny poems (well, at least not serious!) about you, your friends, or a famous person.

For example, if I were going to write a Clerihew about myself, I might write …

Doctor, Doctor, Doctor Dye
Taught her class and wondered why
Not one student made a peep.
Then she saw they'd gone to sleep.

Or, I might write one like this …

Doctor Becky loves to read.
For piles of books she has a need.
But her mother often wishes
She'd take a break and do the dishes.

It's your turn! Write two Clerihews about yourself. Again, do your work in pencil so when you make changes, it will be quick and neat. When you are finished, share your poems with at least three others in your class. Since you know your classmates so well, decide who wrote the funniest Clerihew.

1. _____
   _____
   _____
   _____

2. _____
   _____
   _____
   _____

© Mark Twain Media, Inc., Publishers

Poetry Writing   Chapter Five: *The Clerihew*

Name: _____ Date: _____

Chapter Five: *The Clerihew*

Now pick two friends and write Clerihews about them. Your friends can be classmates, neighbors, or people younger or older than you. Remember, these people are your friends. They should be able to enjoy the poem as much as you do. (You can be funny *and* polite! The point is NOT to embarrass people!)

1. _____
   _____
   _____
   _____

2. _____
   _____
   _____
   _____

Think about a famous person you have discussed in social studies. For example, I might write one about George Washington.

President George Washington
Must have been a model son.
Chopped that tree and didn't lie.
He'd do anything for cherry pie!

I might write one about Noah Webster this way ...

Noah Webster's dictionary
Keeps my work from being scary.
It tells me if it's blew or blue
Or for or four or to or two.

Poetry Writing   Chapter Five: *The Clerihew*

Name: _____ Date: _____

Chapter Five: *The Clerihew*

Try writing one or two Clerihews about people you've discussed in social studies. It could be a president, an inventor, a scientist, or even a teacher!

1. _____
   _____
   _____
   _____

2. _____
   _____
   _____
   _____

Think about a character or two on one of your favorite television programs and try capturing those characters in Clerihews.

1. _____
   _____
   _____
   _____

2. _____
   _____
   _____
   _____

Poetry Writing

Name: _____ Date: _____

Chapter Five: *The Clerihew*

Think about a favorite music group or even a character in a book you have just finished. Try writing a Clerihew about several people in these.

1. _____
   _____
   _____
   _____

2. _____
   _____
   _____
   _____

3. _____
   _____
   _____
   _____

Share your Clerihews with your class. Did any of you choose the same characters from TV, music, or books? If you chose the same characters, how similar were your Clerihews?

Copy your best Clerihew (or attach the paper on which you wrote it) in this space. That way, you'll keep track of your best work.

_____
_____
_____
_____

Chapter Six: *The Ballad*

The next kind of poem we will try writing is the **ballad**. The ballad is an old, old form of poetry that can be sung. Long ago, back before most people could read or write, storytelling and listening were very popular pastimes. During the Middle Ages, some storytellers played music while they told their tales. Minstrels (musical storytellers) actually turned the stories into songs and sang them. These ballads became extremely popular because their simple language, rhyme, and rhythm made them easy to remember. These ballads also usually had several lines that repeated—a chorus. When an audience had heard the chorus several times, they would often sing it right along with the minstrel. Later, some ballads were written down and were really meant to be read, not sung. They were called **literary** ballads. They are *literary* because they were more like *literature* (stories) than songs.

What were these ballads about? Ballads were (and still are) written about brave deeds; happy, sad, or silly events; historical events; make-believe legends; and even romances. Regardless of topic, ballads usually end by teaching some kind of truth or lesson: we should not talk to strangers, we should not spend our money before we have it, sometimes a three-hour tourist cruise *can* take *MUCH* longer, and so on. So even silly ballads can and often do have serious moments.

You may have heard or read ballads about Casey Jones, Paul Bunyon, Robin Hood, or Barbara Allen. Look through your language arts or literature book to see which are included.

How difficult is it to write a ballad? Remember, a ballad is a story that is told in such a way that it probably could be sung. Most songs will have a regular rhythm, regular rhyme, and a chorus. So writing a ballad is a challenge, but if I can do it, you can do it.

Here is a ballad I've created about a boy named Morris and a girl named Daisy. My ballad tells a story told in lines that have both regular rhythm and predictable (you know it's coming) rhyme. My ballad is written in four-line stanzas called quatrains. (Remember quatrains?) Words at the ends of lines two and four will rhyme. When words at the ends of the lines rhyme, we call it **end** rhyme. Every once in a while, I will also include something called an **internal** rhyme: one or more words in a line will rhyme.

I have also numbered each line so after you have read the ballad, I can call your attention to some things I don't want you to miss. Usually, poets don't number their lines.

(1) I've a story to tell you, a story of love,
(2) But a story of sadness, of woe,
(3) Even now I am crying, I'm sobbing, I'm sighing,
(4) Oh, Morris, I feel for you so!

(5) Morris was a fine fellow, so honest and true.
(6) He won medals in spelling and math.
(7) But his writing was sloppy, his hair, like a mop, he
(8) Had never made neatness his path.

Chapter Six: *The Ballad*

OH ...
 (9) A chorus for Morris, a chorus for Morris
(10) A chorus for Morris, ho hum ...,
(11) One more chorus for Morris, a chorus for Morris
(12) Well, I think this chorus is dumb.

(13) Messy Morris met Daisy who was never lazy.
(14) Her papers were perfectly neat.
(15) She did homework in ink and well, just as you'd think
(16) She sat perfectly straight in her seat.

But ...
(17) When it came to jump rope, that Daisy had no hope.
(18) She thought it might mess up her hair.
(19) When the others were playing, inside she was staying.
(20) No, she wasn't going out there!

OH,
(21) A chorus for Morris, a chorus for Morris
(22) A chorus for Morris, ho hum ...,
(23) One more chorus for Morris, a chorus for Morris
(24) Well, I think this chorus is dumb.

(25) "I love you, dear Daisy, but Daisy, you're crazy.
(26) Run and jump, girl, get physically fit.
(27) Get healthy, be strong, and your life will be long."
(28) Well, Daisy went into a snit.

(29) "Morris, you're a mess and what's more I confess
(30) Your hairstyle leaves much to desire
(31) Your papers aren't straight, and at lunchtime you ate
(32) Like a monkey whose tail was on fire."

OH,
(33) A chorus for Morris, a chorus for Morris
(34) A chorus for Morris, ho hum ...,
(35) One more chorus for Morris, a chorus for Morris
(36) Well, I think this chorus is dumb.

(37) Now in unhappy ending, a message I'm sending
(38) To all who will hear this sad song.
(39) Wash your face. Take a hike. Find someone that you like,
(40) Here's the chorus. Now, just sing along.

Chapter Six: *The Ballad*

> (41) *A chorus for Morris, a chorus for Morris*
> (42) *A chorus for Morris, ho hum …,*
> (43) *One more chorus for Morris, a chorus for Morris*
> (44) *Well, I think this chorus is dumb.*

Did you figure out which lines are the chorus? (Of chorus!)

Did you find the lines with internal rhyme? Take your pencil, and reread the poem. Using a pencil so you can quickly erase your mistakes, make a very *light* line under the words that demonstrate internal rhyme. (Go ahead. I'll wait …)

Okay! Let's see how you did. In line three, you should underline *crying* and *sighing*. In line seven, you underline *sloppy* and *mop, he*. (Yeah, that one was a little tricky.) In every chorus, you underline *chorus* and *Morris*. In line 13, underline *Daisy* and *lazy*. In line 15, the underlined words are *ink* and *think*. In line 17, underline *rope* and *hope*, and in line 19, underline *playing* and *staying*. In line 25, the words are *Daisy, Daisy,* and *crazy*. In line 27, the words are *strong* and *long*. In line 29, the words are *mess* and *confess*. In line 31, the words are *straight* and *ate*. In line 37, the words are *ending* and *sending*. And in line 39 (talk about internal rhyme!!), the words are *like* and *hike*. I hope you found all of them! You don't always find internal rhyme in every ballad, but sometimes poets use it to help the reader (or singer) to keep the ballad from going too slow or too fast.

This next part is really tricky. It will ask you to remember something from the last chapter. Are you up to it?

Remember I said to make a light line under the internal rhyme? Now I want you to make some light squiggly lines (or, if you have a colored pencil, use it) and underline (squiggly) the words or parts of words in each line that have the beat—words you tend to emphasize when you read. Go ahead. I'll wait!)

What kind of beat pattern or patterns did you find? Which kind did you find the most?

Were most of the patterns *iambic*? (daw dee) (u /) ex: amount
Were most of the patterns *trochaic*? (dee daw) (/ u) ex: peanut
Were most of the patterns *dactylic*? (dee daw daw) (/ u u) ex: butterfly
Were most of the patterns *anapestic*? (daw daw dee) (u u /) ex: pioneer
Were most of the patterns *spondee*? (dee dee) (/ /) ex: hobo

If you had trouble figuring out the beat pattern, don't be worried. Poets usually begin writing, and the words eventually begin to fit the beat. If a word doesn't work right or *feel* right, the poet just thinks until the right word comes along. A poet DOES NOT think, "Oh, my. I need a word that is dactylic. What word do I know that is dactylic?"

Poetry Writing

Chapter Six: *The Ballad*

Oh yes ... I turned the nouns (iambus, trochee, etc.) into adjectives: words that describe something. So, an iambus becomes an iambic pattern. A trochee becomes a trochaic pattern, and so on. Did you notice that change? Good for you!

We usually only use words like iambic, dactylic, anapestic, and spondaic when we are talking about finished poems. It is helpful to be able to say things like, "On line 24, the poet changes the pattern from the iambic to the trochaic and ends with a spondee. That change makes the poem read very roughly. But, since the poem is describing roller-skating on cracked concrete, the poet uses words that make me feel every bump and crack."

If you are not comfortable talking about iambic and trochaic and so on, don't worry. This book is about writing poems much more than it is about discussing a poet's finished poems. (By the way, I would say that most lines in my ballad about Morris and Daisy have a trochaic pattern.)

Do you think you are ready to try writing a ballad? Let me make a few suggestions that might help you.

First, think of a fairy tale you know very, very well. Then, on your own paper, write just a summary of the story. You don't need to write every little detail, but you will need to tell enough to hit the highlights. I suggest you do this (like all of your practice writing) in pencil.

Once you have the important parts remembered and jotted down, try telling that story in four-line stanzas. Don't worry about a rhythm pattern when you start, but do try to make your second and fourth lines rhyme.

If that doesn't work, see if this helps. Fill in the blanks and good luck.

Oh a long time _____ in a land far away,

Lived a youngster the stories call _____.

With her basket of _____ she skipped down the path

"I'll take Granny some _____," she said.

(Did that get you started? If not, try this one.)

With a fee and a _____ and a foe and a _____

Magic _____ were the payment to _____

For his old weary cow. Those beans sprouted and how!

_____ climbed up them to never look back.

Chapter Six: *The Ballad*

(Hmm. What about ...)

The story of poor _____
Is such a sad, sad tale.
For breaking into Three Bears' house,
She spent some time in _____.

(Hey, I'm doing my best here! Are you writing yet?)

Don't forget that even light or funny ballads have serious moments. Many ballads are very serious from their beginnings to their ends. You may want to try putting a very serious story into a very serious ballad.

This might be part of a very serious ballad.

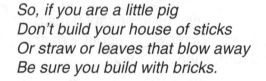

So, if you are a little pig
Don't build your house of sticks
Or straw or leaves that blow away
Be sure you build with bricks.

Or if you are a big bad wolf,
Who likes to scheme or snoop.
Don't slide down chimneys unannounced.
You could wind up in soup!

Now it is your turn! Your ballad can be funny or serious. It can be short or long. But it must tell a story, it should have a regular pattern of words that rhyme, and it should have a fairly regular beat or rhythm. It should also have a chorus—remember Morris?

Don't expect to sit down and write your whole ballad in ten minutes! If you get "stuck," take a break or find someone to read your work and make suggestions. Even if you do write the whole thing at once, don't be surprised if when you see it again in a day or two, you want to make changes. That's why I suggest you always write in pencil until you get the words just the way you want them. When the words are just right, copy your ballad on the lines provided or tape your finished work on the next page.

Name: _____ Date: _____

Chapter Six: *The Ballad*

Ballad Title: _____

Chapter Seven: *Concrete Poems*

Let's take a break from long poems that have more structured rhythm and rhyme. Poets sometimes choose other ways to make even simple words do very hard work. Don't forget: poets not only control the words they choose, but they also control how the words and the lines are arranged. They can even make their poems look like what they are discussing/describing, even if they only use one word! (I told you poets were powerful people!) Take a look at a special kind of poem called a **concrete poem**.

A concrete poem is created by using the word or words in the poem to draw a picture of the topic of the poem. The picture or shape of the poem will show the action, the sound the topic makes, or even the meaning of the words in the poem. Here is my concrete poem called **"Star."**

S
TAR
STAR
STARST
ARSTARST
ARSTARSTAR
STARSTARSTARS
TARSTARSTARSTAR
STARSTARSTARSTARSTAR
STARSTARSTARSTARSTARSTARSTAR
STARSTARSTARSTARSTARSTARSTARSTARSTARS
TARSTARSTARSTARSTARSTARSTARSTA
RSTARSTARSTARSTARSTAR
STARSTARSTARSTARSTARS
TARSTARSTARSTARS
TARSTARSTARS
TARSTARSTA
RSTARSTAR
STARSTA
RSTAR
STA
R

Chapter Seven: *Concrete Poems*

A concrete poem may also be a sentence or two written in the shape of the poem's topic. Here is my poem, **"Knife, Fork, and Spoon."**

Buttered toast is delicious. Sliced carrots ... carved turkey. Please cut my meat for me! Beautifully swirled jelly in a peanut butter sandwich—knife art. Pretty sharp, huh?

                                                      a fork, but I think

There are many things I like to eat with   that my favorite

                                                         is chocolate cake.

                                                 tain of potato

I slurp soup, stir ice tea, scoop a dent in a moun   es

                                                for Lake Gravy.

Now it's your turn. Try creating at least one of both kinds of concrete poems: a word that is repeated in the shape of itself and a sentence or two that is lined out in the shape of the topic. Write the poems on your own paper. Copy or attach your two best poems on the next page.

Poetry Writing

Name: _____ Date: _____

Chapter Seven: *Concrete Poems*

Copy or attach your two best concrete poems in the space below.

Chapter Eight: *The Limerick*

Now that you've had a break from structured rhythm and rhyme, you'll be ready to jump right back into it and try writing a **limerick**.

Limericks have been around a long time, but exactly how long, no one knows for sure. Some people think that limericks might have been like choruses from songs sung by people who lived in the town of Limerick, Ireland. Still, no one seems to know for sure.

There are some things that we do know about limericks and are very sure about. For instance, a limerick has five lines. A limerick has a very precise rhyme pattern: lines one, two, and five must rhyme, and lines three and four must rhyme. Also, a limerick has a definite rhythm pattern: it is anapestic. What's more, a limerick has *feet*.

What? A poem has feet?

Yes, and many with feet stand alone! Now, let me explain what I mean by a poem having feet.

Feet in a poem refers to a rhythmic unit. If you remember, back in the first chapter of this book, you looked at the different rhythm patterns and identified the iambus (iambic), trochee (trochaic), dactyl (dactylic), anapest (anapestic), and spondee (spondaic) patterns. There are a few others, but these are the main ones.

We are now going to count the number of units (how many times that rhythmic pattern repeats) in each line.

If we find only one unit, we call it **monometer**. It has only one foot. It would look like this.

Alone.

There is only one word in the line. It's pattern (*u /*) is iambic. So I would say that that line has **iambic monometer**. It has only one unit of the iambic rhythm pattern.

If we find a line that reads, *"Alone. Alone …,"* it would have two units of the iambic pattern. I would say that it had **iambic dimeter**.

You guessed it! A line that has three sets of the iambic pattern would have what is called **iambic trimeter**.

A line that has four sets of the iambic pattern would have what is called **iambic tetrameter**.

A line that has five sets of the iambic pattern would have what is called **iambic pentameter**.

A line that has six sets of the iambic pattern would have what is called **iambic hexameter**.

A line that has seven sets of the iambic pattern would have what is called **iambic heptameter**.

Remember:

Mono	+	meter	=	one foot
Di	+	meter	=	two feet
Tri	+	meter	=	three feet
Tetra	+	meter	=	four feet
Penta	+	meter	=	five feet
Hexa	+	meter	=	six feet
Hepta	+	meter	=	seven feet

Chapter Eight: *The Limerick*

So if you read a line of poetry and found four units of trochee, you would say the poem had ... **trochaic tetrameter**.

If you read a line of poetry and found three units of spondee, you would say the poem had ... **spondaic trimeter**.

If you read a line of poetry and found six units of dactyl, you would say the poem had ... **dactylic hexameter**.

If you read a line of poetry and found seven units of anapest, you would say that the poem had ... **anapestic heptameter**.

Way to go! Now that you know the words, let's see if you can apply those words.

When we started discussing the limerick, we said that there were several things that a limerick simply must have.

First, a limerick is a light and funny poem. It is not supposed to be a gross or embarrassing poem. If you are going to write a limerick, it should be the kind that everyone—from your best buddy to the school principal—should be able to read, smile, and enjoy.

Second, a limerick needs to have five lines. Lines *one, two,* and *five* must have the same end rhyme. Lines *three* and *four* must have the same end rhyme.

Now here is the tricky part. Lines *one, two,* and *five* should have three units each of anapestic rhythm—**anapestic trimeter**. Lines *three* and *four* should have two units each of anapestic rhythm—**anapestic dimeter**.

What does all that mean in English? It means that the rhythm will sound and feel like the one you are about to read. The example limerick has only two words: *daw* and *dee*. Let's keep things fairly simple to start! (Read this out loud, and remember to emphasize/stress the *dee* parts. Thanks!)

(1)   Daw daw dee   daw daw dee   daw daw dee ...

(2)   Daw daw dee   daw daw dee   daw daw dee.

(3)   Daw daw dee   daw daw dee.

(4)   Daw daw dee   daw daw dee.

(5)   Daw daw dee   daw daw dee   daw daw dee.

Notice that lines one, two, and five are anapestic trimeter. Notice that lines three and four are anapestic dimeter.

Chapter Eight: *The Limerick*

Now I'm going to try and actually put words to it in place of the *daw* and *dee.* Here goes!

(1) I feel sad for that old Dr. Dye.
(2) She taught class and then she wondered why
(3) No one let out a peep
(4) Well, they'd all gone to sleep.
(5) And the shock of the snores made her cry.

Let's check to make sure it meets the rules. Lines one, two, and five have anapestic trimeter. Lines three and four have anapestic dimeter. Lines one, two, and five have end rhyme. Lines three and four have end rhyme.

Get the idea? Here is another one.

(1) Doctor Becky, she sure loves to read.
(2) For those big books, she sure has a need.
(3) Doc's mother sure wishes
(4) She'd just do the dishes.
(5) And she wishes she'd do them with speed.

Okay, check it out. Lines one, two, and five have anapestic trimeter. They also have end rhyme. Lines three and four have anapestic dimeter. They also have end rhyme.

Well, that's enough about me! How about this limerick about George Washington. (It is very much like a Clerihew I wrote earlier in this book!)

(1) Give a cheer for old George Washington.
(2) He was certainly one model son.
(3) He sure chopped down that tree,
(4) But between you and me,
(5) He ate his cherry pie on the run!

Can you stand one more example? (How do your feet feel?)

(1) Thank goodness for my dictionary.
(2) It keeps my work from being scary.
(3) It says blue *is not* blew.
(4) Four's *not* for, two's *not* too.
(5) This word stuff can really be hairy!

Poetry Writing   Chapter Eight: *The Limerick*

Name: _____ Date: _____

Chapter Eight: *The Limerick*

Are you ready to start writing a limerick? (Please start so I can stop!)

Good luck, and when you have one ready, share it with at least three people in your class. Listen to how it sounds when your limerick is read OUT LOUD. Sometimes we need to hear someone else read our poems out loud to be sure we haven't left out any words or to be sure we have the emphasis on the right syllables … Also, let your teacher read your limerick!

After you've written several on your own paper, copy or attach a few of your best limericks in the space below.

_____
_____
_____
_____
_____
_____
_____
_____
_____
_____
_____
_____
_____
_____
_____
_____
_____

Chapter Nine: *The Sonnet*

Probably the most challenging poem you will be asked to write is a **sonnet**. Most believe that the sonnet came from Italy because in Italian, *sonnet* means "little sound." We also tend to think that the first sonnets were either recited with musical accompaniment (some kind of stringed instrument) or actually may have been sung. We also know that the sonnet is a fairly old form of poetry with examples going back to A.D. 1200. Petrarch was probably the most famous of the Italians to write sonnets.

In the 1500s, people in England became really fascinated with sonnets. Even though they wrote them *in English,* poets called them *Italian sonnets* because the form came from Italy. Later, the English poets (such as Shakespeare) continued to write sonnets, but because he changed the length of the lines as well as which lines rhymed, we have a second kind of sonnet called the *Shakespearean* or *English sonnet.* Finally, a third kind of sonnet grew out of the English sonnet, the *Spencerian sonnet.* Again, the difference is mainly in the length of the lines and which line rhymes with which.

Well, if a sonnet was probably sung, how is it different from a ballad, which was also probably sung?

You are just full of really good questions!

First, a sonnet NEVER has more than 14 lines. It doesn't make any difference if it is an Italian, an English, or a Spencerian sonnet. There is no rule that says anything about how many lines are required to make a ballad. Furthermore, a ballad tells a *story.* A sonnet tells more about an *idea* or a *thought* than a story.

Next, a ballad can have just about any kind of beat (meter) or rhyme pattern. A sonnet has very strict rules about that, and yes, you guessed it, there are strict rules for writing an Italian, English, or a Spencerian sonnet. So if you are going to play the game (and writing a sonnet is much like playing a complicated game), you need to learn the rules.

Let's start with the Italian sonnet since it came first.

Rule One:

Like all sonnets, an **Italian sonnet** has 14 lines. It tells its story or asks its question in the first eight lines called an *octave* (awk-tave). Then it tells a kind of lesson about the story or answers its question in the last six lines called a *sestet* (ses-tet). You've heard words like octave and sestet before. If two people sing or play instruments together, it is called a duet. If three sing or play instruments, it is called a trio. When four sing or play instruments, it is called a quartet. When five sing or play instruments, it is called a quintet. Well, a sextet involves six, and an octet involves eight. So a sestet involves six lines, and an octave involves eight lines. See, you knew this all along!

Chapter Nine: *The Sonnet*

Rule Two:

Italian sonnets are almost always written in *iambic pentameter.* That means that we will find the iambic pattern (*u /*) or (*daw dee*) five times (pentameter) per line.

Rule Three:

Italian sonnets have a predictable rhyme pattern. Up to now, we have talked about short groups of lines—couplets (two lines), tercets (three lines), and quatrains (four lines). Since we are talking about longer *groups* of lines, we find it easier to discuss the patterns the following way.

In an Italian sonnet, the *octave* (first group of eight lines) has a pattern of *abbaabba.* That means that the lines will rhyme like this:

line one:	We call the last word in this line rhyme *a.*
line two:	We call the last word in this line rhyme *b.*
	It will NOT rhyme with line one!
line three:	Because this line will rhyme with line two, we call it rhyme *b.*
line four:	Because this line will rhyme with line one, we call it rhyme *a.*
line five:	Because this line will rhyme with line one, we call it rhyme *a.*
line six:	Because this line will rhyme with line two, we call it rhyme *b.*
line seven:	Because this line will rhyme with line two, we call it rhyme *b.*
line eight:	Because this line will rhyme with line one, we call it rhyme *a.*

The *abbaabba* pattern means that lines *one, four, five,* and *eight* must rhyme with each other. It also means that lines *two, three, six,* and *seven* must rhyme with each other.

Are you still with me? Good! We are nearly finished.

Now, let's figure out the last six lines—the sestet. The rhyme pattern for the sestet is usually *cdccdc.* Sometimes it is *cdedce,* but for right now, let's put *cdedce* on hold.

All this means that we set up our last six lines to rhyme like this if we use *cdccdc* like most sestets do.

line nine:	The last word uses a new end word with a rhyme called *c.*
line ten:	The last word uses a new end word with a rhyme called *d.*
line eleven:	This line must rhyme with line nine called *c.*
line twelve:	This line must rhyme with line nine called *c.*
line thirteen:	This line must rhyme with line ten called *d.*
line fourteen:	This line must rhyme with line nine called *c.*

In other words, lines *nine, eleven, twelve,* and *fourteen* must rhyme with each other. Lines *ten* and *thirteen* must rhyme with each other.

Chapter Nine: *The Sonnet*

That's it. Now look at and listen to an Italian sonnet that I wrote. I'll underline the stressed beats so you can count five in each line, and I'll put the *abbaabbacdccdc* pattern at the end of each line. Check to make sure I didn't goof!

(1) And <u>what</u> do <u>I</u> want <u>now</u> to <u>eat</u> for <u>lunch</u>?   (a)
(2) My <u>stom</u>ach <u>is</u> so <u>emp</u>ty <u>I</u> could <u>die</u>.   (b)
(3) I'd <u>real</u>ly <u>love</u> to <u>or</u>der <u>piz</u>za <u>pie</u>.   (b)
(4) Ba<u>nan</u>as? <u>I</u> know <u>I</u> could <u>eat</u> a <u>bunch</u>.   (a)
(5) By <u>now</u>, I <u>think</u> that <u>you</u> would <u>have</u> a <u>hunch</u>   (a)
(6) That <u>if</u> I <u>don't</u> eat <u>soon</u>, you'll <u>start</u> to <u>cry</u>.   (b)
(7) Be<u>cause</u> you <u>end</u>ed <u>up</u> with <u>a</u> black <u>eye</u>.   (b)
(8) Pro<u>vide</u> some <u>food</u> or <u>I</u> will <u>throw</u> a <u>punch</u>.   (a)
(9) The <u>prob</u>lem <u>here</u> is <u>ve</u>ry <u>plain</u> to <u>see</u>.   (c)
(10) I <u>over</u>slept and <u>had</u> no <u>break</u>fast <u>meal</u>.   (d)
(11) With<u>out</u> some <u>food</u>, a <u>mon</u>ster <u>I</u> can <u>be</u>.   (c)
(12) I <u>might</u> go <u>on</u> a <u>great</u> big <u>eat</u>ing <u>spree</u>.   (c)
(13) So <u>let</u> me <u>know</u> right <u>now</u>. Please <u>make</u> a <u>deal</u>. (d)
(14) And <u>share</u> your <u>can</u>dy <u>bar</u> with <u>starv</u>ing <u>me</u>! (c)

There you have an Italian sonnet. It is a 14-lined poem written in iambic pentameter. The 14 lines are arranged into an octave (a group of eight lines) and a sestet (a group of six lines). The octave has a rhyme pattern of *abbaabba,* and the sestet has a rhyme pattern of *cdccdc.* The octave tells a story, and the sestet provides a kind of lesson: when I oversleep and don't eat any breakfast, I just might come begging for your candy bar!

Poetry Writing   Chapter Nine: *The Sonnet*

Name:_____ Date:_____

Chapter Nine: *The Sonnet*

It's your turn! Try writing an Italian sonnet (in pencil!) on these lines.

_____
_____
_____
_____
_____
_____
_____
_____
_____
_____
_____
_____
_____
_____

Great job!

Chapter Nine: *The Sonnet*

Are you ready for the rules to "play" (write) an English or Shakespearean sonnet? Here they are.

Rule One:

Like all sonnets, an English sonnet has 14 lines. Like the Italian sonnet, the English sonnet tells a brief story, discusses an idea, or asks you to think about a question. Then the last few lines of the sonnet teach a lesson, make a comment, or answer the question it asked. But unlike the Italian sonnet with its octave and sestet, the English sonnet puts its 14 lines into *three quatrains* (three stanzas of four lines each) and *one couplet* (two lines). The three quatrains give the story/question/idea, and the couplet makes the comment.

Rule Two:

Like Italian sonnets, the English sonnet is usually written in iambic pentameter. That means that we will find the iambic pattern (*u /*) or (*daw dee*) five times (pentameter) per line.

Rule Three:

English sonnets have their own kind of rhyme pattern: *abab cdcd efef gg*. When we put these letters on lines of real poetry, it goes like this:

Quatrain (stanza with four lines) #1

line one:	The last word in this line we'll call *a*.
line two:	The last word in this line we'll call *b*.
line three:	The last word in this line will rhyme with *a*.
line four:	The last word in this line will rhyme with *b*.

Quatrain #2

line five:	The last word in this line we'll call *c*. (It doesn't rhyme with *a* or *b*.)
line six:	The last word in this line we'll call *d*.
line seven:	The last word in this line rhymes with *c*.
line eight:	The last word in this line rhymes with *d*.

Chapter Nine: *The Sonnet*

Quatrain #3

　　line nine:　　　The last word in this line we'll call *e*.
　　　　　　　　　(It doesn't rhyme with *a*, *b*, *c*, or *d*.)
　　line ten:　　　The last word in this line we'll call *f*.
　　line eleven:　　The last word in this line rhymes with *e*.
　　line twelve:　　The last word in this line rhymes with *f*.

Now, we finish with the couplet.

　　line thirteen: The last word in this line we'll call *g*.
　　line fourteen: The last word in this line rhymes with *g*.

So do the math! Three *quatrains* (three groups of four lines) plus a *couplet* (two lines) equals 14 lines. Lines one and three rhyme. Lines two and four rhyme. Lines five and seven rhyme. Lines six and eight rhyme. Lines nine and eleven rhyme. Lines ten and twelve rhyme, and lines thirteen and fourteen rhyme. Taa Daa!

That's it. Now look and listen to an English sonnet that I wrote. I'll underline the stressed beats for you to count five iambs in each line, and I'll put the *abab*, etc. patterns at the end of each line. Check to make sure I didn't goof!

(1)	*When Christopher Columbus was in school,*	(a)
(2)	*They thought they knew for sure the world was flat.*	(b)
(3)	*When he grew up, they thought he was a fool*	(a)
(4)	*For challenging their law, and that was that.*	(b)
(5)	*When Lindbergh flew his plane across the sea,*	(c)
(6)	*They said that he was wrong to try the flight.*	(d)
(7)	*A silly man that Lindbergh sure must be!*	(c)
(8)	*To fly across the ocean isn't right.*	(d)
(9)	*So now it's up to you to lead the way*	(e)
(10)	*To challenge notions new and notions old.*	(f)
(11)	*Just think! You might invent something today.*	(e)
(12)	*Don't be afraid! Be strong. Be brave. Be bold.*	(f)
(13)	*The time is right. The choice belongs to you.*	(g)
(14)	*The world is yours and now, what will you do?*	(g)

Chapter Nine: *The Sonnet*

Try writing an English (Shakespearean) sonnet.

Poetry Writing   Chapter Nine: *The Sonnet*

Name: _____ Date: _____

Chapter Nine: *The Sonnet*

Last, but not least, is the Spencerian sonnet. It is just like the English sonnet except it has a different rhyme pattern. It is called an *interlocking* pattern because all the quatrains will share rhyme. This is the pattern: *abab   bcbc   cdcd   ee.*

This is an example of a Spencerian sonnet.

(1)	A <u>sonnet</u> <u>can</u> be <u>difficult</u> to <u>write</u>.	(a)
(2)	It's <u>hard</u> to <u>make</u> the <u>rhyme</u> and <u>rhythm</u> <u>fit</u>.	(b)
(3)	It <u>makes</u> me <u>tired</u> … my <u>head</u> and <u>shoulders</u> <u>tight</u>.	(a)
(4)	I <u>get</u> so <u>mad</u> I <u>often</u> <u>want</u> to <u>quit</u>.	(b)
(5)	And <u>then</u>, I <u>stop</u> and <u>take</u> a <u>look</u> at <u>it</u>.	(b)
(6)	I <u>know</u> that <u>I</u> have <u>done</u> my <u>ver</u>-y <u>best</u>.	(c)
(7)	And <u>I</u> <u>know</u> <u>that</u> it's <u>read</u>-y to submit.	(b)
(8)	Its <u>rhyme</u> and <u>rhythm</u> <u>passes</u> <u>ev</u>'ry <u>test</u>.	(c)
(9)	It's <u>time</u> for <u>me</u> to <u>go</u> to <u>bed</u> and <u>rest</u>.	(c)
(10)	But <u>when</u> I <u>close</u> my <u>eyes</u> to <u>go</u> to <u>sleep</u>	(d)
(11)	<u>I</u>ambic <u>patterns</u> <u>pound</u> with<u>in</u> my <u>chest</u>.	(c)
(12)	I <u>count</u> pent<u>am</u>eters in<u>stead</u> of <u>sheep</u>.	(d)
(13)	I <u>never</u> <u>want</u> to <u>write</u> <u>another</u> <u>one</u>.	(e)
(14)	And <u>I'm</u> the <u>fool</u> who <u>thought</u> this <u>would</u> be <u>fun</u>!	(e)

Now I dare you to write a Spencerian sonnet!

_____
_____
_____
_____
_____
_____
_____
_____
_____
_____
_____
_____
_____

Chapter Nine: *The Sonnet*

After writing several sonnets of each kind, copy or attach your best sonnet in the space below.

Chapter Ten: *The Haiku (Gesundheit!)*

After writing a sonnet, you must be exhausted. Now would be a good time to try writing a haiku: a poem with three lines that does not rhyme.

From the title of this chapter, you might think that haiku is the sound of someone sneezing. Nothing could be further from the truth.

A **haiku** is an old form of Japanese poetry that poets worldwide "discovered" in the early 1900s. A haiku has only three lines and does not rhyme, but it does have one rule: you must have the right number of syllables in each line.

THE RULE: The first line must have five syllables, the second line must have seven syllables, and the third line must have five syllables.

That's it! The haiku depends on a very few carefully chosen words to do a very big job. Are you up to the task?

Here are a few examples of haiku.

(1)	The Fourth of July	(5 syllables)
(2)	Bands and parades and fireworks	(7 syllables)
(3)	Lemonade and fun	(5 syllables)

(1)	I'm doing my math.	(5 syllables)
(2)	I'm counting on my fingers.	(7 syllables)
(3)	I still don't get it.	(5 syllables)

(1)	The birds now sing spring.	(5 syllables)
(2)	The grass is starting to green.	(7 syllables)
(3)	Winter is over.	(5 syllables)

Haikus can tell little stories, describe an image, or just list reactions. You can use sentences, or you can simply select words that create the sound of what you feel.

Poetry Writing

Name: _____ Date: _____

Chapter Ten: *The Haiku*

It's your turn to write.

1. Write a haiku about a season of the year.

   _____
   _____
   _____

2. Try a haiku about a pet or a wild animal.

   _____
   _____
   _____

3. Try a haiku about spaghetti.

   _____
   _____
   _____

4. Try a haiku about a library.

   _____
   _____
   _____

5. Finish with a haiku on mud.

   _____
   _____
   _____

Chapter Eleven: *The Biopoem*

Here is another kind of poem that will not ask the poet to think of words that rhyme. However, it will ask for some definite information in a definite order. It was developed by A. Gere as a way to help students learn and remember information about individuals.

The **biopoem** is a short biography—nine lines of specific information about a person. The person could be a historical figure, a cartoon character, a person who gives the weather forecast on TV, or even yourself.

All you need to do is fill in the blanks!

Line one: State the name of the person.

Line two: List four words that describe that person.

Line three: State where (country, city) or when (time period) the person lives or lived.

Line four: List three things that the person likes.

Line five: List three things the person feels or thinks.

Line six: List three things the person needs to be happy.

Line seven: List three things the person fears.

Line eight: List three important things the person has done or is responsible for.

Line nine: Give a synonym for the person—a one-word description for who or what that person is.

Here is a biopoem I've written. Look how each line tells specific information about the person.

Line 1 Name	*Dr. Rebecca L. Dye*
Line 2 Four words describing	*Ambitious Reserved Nervous Calm*
Line 3 Country/time period	*21st Century American*
Line 4 Enjoys (3 things)	*Enjoys Reading, Writing, Shopping*
Line 5 Feels (3 emotions)	*Feels Frustrated Tired Exhilarated*
Line 6 Needs (list 3)	*Needs Love Encouragement Chocolate*
Line 7 Fears (3 things)	*Fears Snakes Spiders the Dark*
Line 8 Significant actions taken (3)	*Graduated … Graduated … Graduated!*
Line 9 Synonym	*Teacher*

Poetry Writing   Chapter Eleven: *The Biopoem*

Name: _____ Date: _____

Chapter Eleven: *The Biopoem*

Try writing a biopoem with me! We'll write one on Martin Luther King, Jr.

- Line 1   *Dr. Martin Luther King, Jr.*
- Line 2   *Caring   Thoughtful* _____ _____
- Line 3   *20th Century American*
- Line 4   *Enjoyed Family, Work, and* _____
- Line 5   *Felt Commitment,* _____ *, and* _____
- Line 6   *Needed Freedom,* _____ *, and* _____
- Line 7   *Feared Failure,* _____ *, and* _____
- Line 8   *Stood for freedom   Jailed for freedom   Died for freedom*
- Line 9   _____

On this page and the next, try writing three biopoems: one about yourself, one about a person in the news right now, and one about someone you've studied in history.

1. Myself

_____
_____
_____
_____
_____
_____
_____
_____

Poetry Writing

Name: _____ Date: _____

Chapter Eleven: *The Biopoem*

2. A person in the news now

   _____
   _____
   _____
   _____
   _____
   _____
   _____
   _____

3. A person in history

   _____
   _____
   _____
   _____
   _____
   _____
   _____
   _____

Chapter Twelve: *The Cinquain*

Like biopoems, **cinquains** have a way of summarizing much information in a limited number of words. And like biopoems, cinquains have fairly strict rules about how many words can be used and in what order information is given. But unlike biopoems, cinquains are not limited to people. In fact, the only thing you can't use as the topic of a cinquain is … a person.

The cinquain was invented by J. Vaughan and T. Estes as a way for students to sort through information so they can understand, remember, and communicate it better. I think it is also a way to write a pretty nifty poem.

Here are the rules!

Line one: Give it a one-word title.

Line two: Write a two-word description of the title/topic.

Line three: Write three action words related to the title/topic.

Line four: Write four words that show feeling for the title/topic.

Line five: Write one word that is a synonym (expresses the same idea) for the title/topic.

Here are a couple of examples I've written.

Line one: *Pancakes*
Line two: *Piping hot*
Line three: *Swimming in syrup*
Line four: *Buttery cakes for breakfast*
Line five: *Flapjacks*

Line one: *Christmas*
Line two: *Universal celebration*
Line three: *Angel choirs sing*
Line four: *Glory in the highest*
Line five: *Birthday*

Poetry Writing　　　　　　　　　　　　　　　　　　　　　Chapter Twelve: *The Cinquain*

Name: _____　Date: _____

Chapter Twelve: *The Cinquain*

Now you try writing a few cinquains. Try writing a cinquain about …

1. … a sport.

   _____
   _____
   _____
   _____
   _____

2. … your favorite food.

   _____
   _____
   _____
   _____
   _____

3. … the town where you live.

   _____
   _____
   _____
   _____
   _____

4. … something you study in science.

   _____
   _____
   _____
   _____
   _____

Chapter Thirteen: *Blank Verse*

Blank verse is a form of poetry in which you will find no rhyming words. However, you will find a very regular rhythm pattern: the iambic pattern. In fact, you will find five iambs (u /) in each line, which means that we would call it … that's right … IAMBIC PENTAMETER!

Some very famous poets wrote important works in blank verse. English poets, such as Shakespeare, Milton, Wordsworth, Keats, and Tennyson, successfully used blank verse. In fact, many of Shakespeare's plays are actually *blank verse:* iambic pentameter that does not rhyme. William Cullen Bryant is one of several American poets who wrote in blank verse. Just think, after a little practice you could add your name to the list.

Here is an example of a poem I wrote in blank verse.

> *I sit and think about what I should do.*
> *I cannot find the words to tell the truth*
> *About today. I won, but didn't say*
> *how awfully sorry and upset I was.*
> *But at the very same time I was glad.*
> *I won our fight and I was glad and yet,*
> *You lost. So now I know that what they say*
> *is false. They say that thrill is what is felt*
> *in victory. I think it's really more*
> *like agony. Who wins? I wish you had.*

I wrote this after watching two people arguing over something that wasn't very important. I started thinking how one person will win only to end up losing something (or someone) far more important. As you read my poem, notice that my sentences don't end at the end of the line. My sentences wrap around to the next line, so that is why I did not begin each line with capital letters or end each line with punctuation. In fact, if I didn't want to put this into ten-syllable lines, I could have written this as a regular paragraph. But there is something very poem-like about this. It means much more than what the words themselves say. Does it remind you of a time you won, but you really lost? (Ah, poets really **are** powerful people!)

Poetry Writing

Name: _____ Date: _____

Chapter Thirteen: *Blank Verse*

Well, it's time for you to flex those mental muscles. Why not try writing a short poem in blank verse about …

… a leaf falling off a tree branch,

… how to eat with chopsticks,

… the way cola fizzes and tickles your nose when you drink from a glass,

… your dog or cat eating its supper,

… riding the school bus home,

… your first recital,

… or something else you'd like to try.

_____
_____
_____
_____
_____
_____
_____
_____
_____
_____
_____
_____
_____

Name: _____ Date: _____

Chapter Fourteen: *Free Verse*

Free verse is poetry that is free of any rules. Free verse has no rules about rhythm or rhyme. Free verse depends on the way the words are put together to make the reader think and feel and experience. But because free verse has no real rules, it is hard to know just how to start writing free verse.

When I hear or see or experience something, I like to try to simply list words that capture what happened. For example, today I was riding in my car and I looked out to see weeds along a fence. The fence was between me and a plowed field. It was a cold, but sunny, March day. To capture that impression, I could list these words: weeds, fence, sun, ice, March.

Now I'll try to put each in a sentence that means a little more than just what the words say in print.

Last fall's weeds lean helplessly, hopelessly against
the rusting fence, their silent friend.
The sun smiles, but tells worthless lies.
Ice rules.
It's March.

Listing words and then writing sentences works best for me, but you may find a different way. There is no right or wrong way to write a poem in free verse!

You try one! Try writing a poem in free verse about … a playground … a gym after a basketball game … a thunderstorm … a snowstorm … your sneakers … a caterpillar inching across a leaf … a fly buzzing around your face …

_____
_____
_____
_____
_____
_____
_____
_____
_____
_____
_____

Name: _____ Date: _____

Chapter Fifteen: *Looking for Ideas and Words That Work*

Where do we find ideas for poems? We get ideas from things we see, things we touch, things we taste, things we smell, things we hear, and things we experience. In other words, we find ideas for poems from being alive and being aware of what is going on around us and inside us. You don't believe me?

For the next 30 seconds, close your eyes. Concentrate on the sounds you hear, the odors you smell, the way your clothes feel from the inside out. Think about how your mouth tastes. Think about the way you feel. Now open your eyes, grab your pencil, and write down as much as you can remember.

_____
_____
_____
_____
_____
_____
_____
_____
_____
_____
_____
_____
_____
_____
_____
_____
_____
_____

Poetry Writing — Name: _____ Date: _____

Chapter Fifteen: *Looking for Ideas and Words That Work*

Close your eyes again. Now think about the room in which you are sitting. Even though your eyes are closed, "see" as much as you can. What is there? What are the colors? What are the textures (rough, smooth, sharp, curved, etc.)? What are the first objects in the room that draw your attention? What is the most interesting feature of the room? Now open your eyes, grab your pencil, and write down as much as you can remember *seeing* with your eyes closed.

_____
_____
_____
_____
_____
_____
_____
_____
_____
_____
_____
_____
_____
_____
_____
_____
_____
_____
_____
_____

Poetry Writing   Chapter Fifteen: *Looking for Ideas and Words That Work*

Name: _____ Date: _____

Chapter Fifteen: *Looking for Ideas and Words That Work*

Finding just the right words to describe what we want to say can be tricky. Sometimes we need to use a dictionary to be sure a word means what we think it means. Sometimes we need a thesaurus, a dictionary of synonyms—words that mean the same thing. Sometimes we simply need to stop and think about what we do know. For example, list as many words as you know that mean the same thing as …

1. big _____
   _____

2. little _____
   _____

3. happy _____
   _____

4. tired _____
   _____

5. hungry _____
   _____

6. mean _____
   _____

7. pretty _____
   _____

8. curious _____
   _____

9. nice _____
   _____

10. awful _____
    _____

11. house _____
    _____

12. car _____
    _____

© Mark Twain Media, Inc., Publishers

Poetry Writing   Chapter Fifteen: *Looking for Ideas and Words That Work*

Name: _____   Date: _____

Chapter Fifteen: *Looking for Ideas and Words That Work*

Now think about other kinds of words—words that when pronounced, say exactly what they mean. We call these words **onomatopoeic** (on-owe-mawt-owe-pee-ic) words.

What? What kind of words?

I said that words having **onomatopoeia** (on-owe-mawt-owe-pee-uh) are words that say what they mean. For example, if you were to accidentally step on a tomato, what sound might that motion make? **Squish? Splat?**

Grab your pencil again, and jot down some onomatopoeic words that could help you say what you want to say **AND** help your poems read and sound better. For example, what would you call the sound of …

1. Fingernails sliding down a chalkboard? _____

2. Tires stopping suddenly on pavement? _____

3. A grandfather clock working away in a quiet room? _____

4. A lion or tiger saying good morning to the world? _____

5. A person eating celery? _____

6. An electric mixer blending ingredients for a cake? _____

7. A bee who thinks you are a flower? _____

8. Waves hitting a sandy beach? _____

9. Waves hitting a rocky beach? _____

10. Bacon frying? _____

11. Windshield wipers? _____

12. An angry cat? _____

13. An approaching thunderstorm? _____

14. A door with rusty hinges? _____

15. A breeze blowing through the leaves of a tree? _____

© Mark Twain Media, Inc., Publishers

Poetry Writing — Chapter Fifteen: *Looking for Ideas and Words That Work*

Name: _____ Date: _____

Chapter Fifteen: *Looking for Ideas and Words That Work*

Poets are *word* people! The more they read, write, and listen, the more words they know and want to use. When was the last time **you** learned a new word? If you haven't learned a new word today, go to the dictionary and find the word *ubiquitous*. Now, how many things can you list that are *ubiquitous*?

_____
_____
_____

While you still have your dictionary handy, look up the word *anfractuous*. How many words can you think of that mean about the same thing as *anfractuous*? (I just learned that word. I *kinda* like it!)

_____
_____
_____

By the way, what does it mean if you eschew something? What kinds of things do you eschew?

_____
_____
_____

Okay, you word nerd! I challenge you to write a poem (any kind you want) that uses the words *ubiquitous, anfractuous,* and *eschew.*

_____
_____
_____
_____
_____
_____
_____

Well, I'm impressed!

© Mark Twain Media, Inc., Publishers

Chapter Sixteen: *Revising and Editing*

As I tell my students, an author (or, in this case, a poet) has one main job: to put words to an idea and put those words in print. An editor is the person who, when the poet has done all he or she can do with the poem, looks over the poem to see if it is ready to share with the audience. Of course, an editor looks to see that a poem measures up to the ordinary rules of spelling, grammar, and punctuation. When you (as the audience) begin to read something that is full of spelling, grammar, and punctuation mistakes, you probably lose interest and just stop reading. You (as the writer) don't want that to happen to your work!

To make sure your work is ready to hand in to your teacher, share with your class, or even send to a publisher to print in a book or magazine, you need to be your own editor first. Ask yourself the following questions.

1. What is this poem supposed to do, and did I achieve my purpose?

2. Are there any errors in spelling, grammar, or punctuation?

3. If I chose a form of poetry that has very strict rules, did I follow them?

4. Did I read my poem out loud to hear the words as well as see the words?

5. Did I use the first word that popped into my head, or did I do some thinking about using a different word, a better word?

6. Did I have anyone else read my poem to make suggestions on how to make it better? More clear? Easier to read?

7. Did I think about who my audience will be? Did I choose a topic and words that they will understand? Find appropriate? Find interesting?

8. Will I be proud to put my name on this poem and share the poem with people I probably do not know?

Poetry Writing — Chapter Sixteen: *Revising and Editing*

Name: _____ Date: _____

Chapter Sixteen: *Revising and Editing*

Copy or attach your best poem(s) here (any kind). Make sure you have edited the poem for spelling, grammar, and punctuation. Also be sure you have followed the rules for the particular type of poem you have written. You will want to read the poem out loud to yourself, and you may want someone else to read the poem and make suggestions before you copy down the final version.

_____
_____
_____
_____
_____
_____
_____
_____
_____
_____
_____
_____
_____
_____
_____
_____
_____
_____
_____
_____
_____
_____